In loving Memory of

_____

_____

Born on

_____

Passed away on

_____

Age

GUESTS

Name

Thoughts and Memories

_____
_____

_____
_____
_____
_____

_____
_____

_____
_____
_____
_____

_____
_____

_____
_____
_____
_____

_____
_____

_____
_____
_____
_____

_____
_____

GUESTS

Name

Thoughts and Memories

GUESTS

Name

Thoughts and Memories

_____

_____

_____

_____

_____

_____

_____

_____

_____

_____

_____

GUESTS

Name

Thoughts and Memories

_____

_____

_____

_____

_____

_____

_____

_____

_____

_____

_____

_____

_____

_____

_____

_____

_____

_____

_____

_____

_____

_____

_____

_____

_____

_____

_____

GUESTS

Name

Thoughts and Memories

GUESTS

Name

Thoughts and Memories

GUESTS

Name

Thoughts and Memories

_____

_____

_____

_____

_____

_____

_____

_____

_____

_____

_____

_____

_____

GUESTS

Name

Thoughts and Memories

GUESTS

Name

Thoughts and Memories

GUESTS

Name

Thoughts and Memories

_____

_____

_____

_____

_____

_____

_____

_____

_____

_____

_____

_____

_____

_____

_____

_____

_____

_____

_____

_____

_____

_____

_____

_____

_____

_____

GUESTS

Name

Thoughts and Memories

_____

_____

_____

_____

_____

GUESTS

Name

Thoughts and Memories

GUESTS

Name

Thoughts and Memories

_____

_____

_____

_____

_____

_____

_____

_____

_____

_____

_____

_____

_____

_____

_____

_____

_____

_____

_____

_____

GUESTS

Name

Thoughts and Memories

GUESTS

Name

Thoughts and Memories

_____

_____

_____

_____

_____

_____

_____

_____

_____

_____

_____

_____

_____

_____

_____

_____

_____

_____

_____

_____

_____

_____

_____

_____

_____

_____

_____

_____

GUESTS

Name

Thoughts and Memories

GUESTS

Name

Thoughts and Memories

GUESTS

Name

Thoughts and Memories

GUESTS

Name

Thoughts and Memories

_____
_____

_____

_____
_____

_____

_____
_____

_____

_____
_____

_____

_____
_____

_____

_____
_____

_____

_____
_____

_____

_____
_____

_____

_____
_____

_____

_____
_____

_____

_____
_____

_____

GUESTS

Name

Thoughts and Memories

_____

_____

_____

_____

_____

_____

_____

_____

_____

_____

_____

_____

_____

_____

_____

_____

_____

_____

_____

_____

_____

_____

_____

_____

_____

GUESTS

Name

Thoughts and Memories

GUESTS

Name

Thoughts and Memories

_____

_____

_____

_____

_____

_____

GUESTS

Name

Thoughts and Memories

GUESTS

Name

Thoughts and Memories

GUESTS

Name

Thoughts and Memories

_____
_____

_____
_____

_____
_____

_____
_____

_____
_____

_____
_____

GUESTS

Name

Thoughts and Memories

_____

_____

_____

_____

_____

_____

_____

_____

_____

_____

_____

_____

_____

_____

_____

_____

_____

_____

_____

_____

_____

_____

_____

_____

_____

_____

_____

GUESTS

Name

Thoughts and Memories

GUESTS

Name

Thoughts and Memories

GUESTS

Name

Thoughts and Memories

GUESTS

Name

Thoughts and Memories

_____

_____

_____

_____

_____

_____

_____

_____

GUESTS

Name

Thoughts and Memories

GUESTS

Name

Thoughts and Memories

_____

_____

_____

_____

_____

_____

_____

_____

_____

_____

_____

_____

_____

_____

_____

_____

_____

_____

_____

_____

_____

_____

_____

_____

_____

_____

_____

_____

_____

_____

GUESTS

Name

Thoughts and Memories

GUESTS

Name

Thoughts and Memories

GUESTS

Name

Thoughts and Memories

GUESTS

Name

Thoughts and Memories

GUESTS

Name

Thoughts and Memories

GUESTS

Name

Thoughts and Memories

GUESTS

Name

Thoughts and Memories

GUESTS

Name

Thoughts and Memories

GUESTS

Name

Thoughts and Memories

GUESTS

Name

Thoughts and Memories

_____

_____

_____

_____

_____

_____

_____

_____

_____

_____

_____

_____

_____

_____

_____

_____

_____

_____

_____

_____

_____

_____

_____

_____

GUESTS

Name

Thoughts and Memories

GUESTS

Name

Thoughts and Memories

GUESTS

Name

Thoughts and Memories

GUESTS

Name

Thoughts and Memories

_____   _____
_____   _____
                                         _____
                                         _____

_____   _____
_____   _____
                                         _____
                                         _____

_____   _____
_____   _____
                                         _____
                                         _____

_____   _____
_____   _____
                                         _____
                                         _____

_____   _____
_____   _____
                                         _____
                                         _____

GUESTS

Name

Thoughts and Memories

_____

_____

_____

_____

_____

_____

_____

_____

_____

_____

_____

_____

_____

_____

_____

_____

_____

_____

_____

_____

_____

_____

_____

_____

_____

_____

_____

_____

_____

GUESTS

Name

Thoughts and Memories

GUESTS

Name

Thoughts and Memories

_____
_____

_____
_____

_____
_____
_____
_____
_____
_____

_____
_____

_____
_____
_____
_____
_____
_____
_____

_____
_____

_____
_____
_____
_____
_____

_____
_____

_____
_____
_____
_____
_____

_____
_____

_____
_____
_____
_____

GUESTS

Name

Thoughts and Memories

GUESTS

Name

Thoughts and Memories

GUESTS

Name

Thoughts and Memories

GUESTS

Name

Thoughts and Memories

GUESTS

Name

Thoughts and Memories

Name

Thoughts and Memories

GUESTS

Name

Thoughts and Memories

GUESTS

Name

Thoughts and Memories

GUESTS

Name

Thoughts and Memories

GUESTS

Name

Thoughts and Memories

GUESTS

Name

Thoughts and Memories

GUESTS

Name

Thoughts and Memories

GUESTS

Name

Thoughts and Memories

GUESTS

Name

Thoughts and Memories

GUESTS

Name

Thoughts and Memories

GUESTS

Name

Thoughts and Memories

GUESTS

Name

Thoughts and Memories

GUESTS

Name

Thoughts and Memories

GUESTS

Name

Thoughts and Memories

_____

_____

_____

_____

_____

_____

_____

_____

_____

_____

_____

_____

_____

_____

_____

_____

_____

_____

_____

_____

_____

_____

GUESTS

Name

Thoughts and Memories

GUESTS

Name

Thoughts and Memories

GUESTS

Name

Thoughts and Memories

GUESTS

Name

Thoughts and Memories

_____

_____

_____

_____

_____

_____

_____

_____

_____

_____

_____

_____

_____

_____

_____

_____

_____

_____

_____

_____

_____

_____

_____

_____

_____

_____

_____

_____

_____

_____

_____

GUESTS

Name

Thoughts and Memories

GUESTS

Name

Thoughts and Memories

_____

_____

_____

_____

_____

_____

_____

_____

_____

_____

_____

_____

_____

_____

_____

_____

_____

_____

_____

_____

_____

_____

_____

GUESTS

Name

Thoughts and Memories

GUESTS

Name

Thoughts and Memories

_____
_____

_____
_____

_____
_____

_____
_____

_____
_____

_____
_____

GUESTS

Name

Thoughts and Memories

GUESTS

Name

Thoughts and Memories

GUESTS

Name

Thoughts and Memories

GUESTS

Name

Thoughts and Memories

GUESTS

Name

Thoughts and Memories

GUESTS

Name

Thoughts and Memories

GUESTS

Name

Thoughts and Memories

GUESTS

Name

Thoughts and Memories

GUESTS

Name

Thoughts and Memories

GUESTS

Name

Thoughts and Memories

_____

_____

_____

_____

_____

_____

_____

_____

_____

_____

_____

_____

_____

_____

_____

_____

_____

_____

_____

_____

_____

_____

_____

_____

_____

GUESTS

Name

Thoughts and Memories

GUESTS

Name

Thoughts and Memories

GUESTS

Name

Thoughts and Memories

GUESTS

Name

Thoughts and Memories

GUESTS

Name

Thoughts and Memories

GUESTS

Name

Thoughts and Memories

GUESTS

Name

Thoughts and Memories

GUESTS

Name

Thoughts and Memories

GUESTS

Name

Thoughts and Memories

GUESTS

Name

Thoughts and Memories

GUESTS

Name

Thoughts and Memories

Printed in Great Britain
by Amazon

2ac2be37-bfb7-426b-ac1b-f61b973ff7c2R01